CHECKING IN

By EMILY ARROW

Illustrations by JOY STEUERWALD

Music by EMILY ARROW

CANTATA
LEARNING

WWW.CANTATALEARNING.COM

CANTATA
LEARNING

Published by Cantata Learning
1710 Roe Crest Drive
North Mankato, MN 56003
www.cantatalearning.com

Copyright © 2020 Cantata Learning

Library of Congress Cataloging-in-Publication Data
Names: Arrow, Emily, author. | Steuerwald, Joy, illustrator.
Title: Checking in / by Emily Arrow ; illustrated by Joy Steuerwald ; music
  by Emily Arrow.
Description: North Mankato, MN : Cantata Learning, [2020] | Series: My
  feelings, my choices | Includes bibliographical references.
Identifiers: LCCN 2018053378 (print) | LCCN 2018055660 (ebook) | ISBN
  9781684104192 (eBook) | ISBN 9781684104048 (hardcover) | ISBN
  9781684104314 (pbk.)
Subjects: LCSH: Calmness--Juvenile literature. | Emotions in
  children--Juvenile literature.
Classification: LCC BF575.C35 (ebook) | LCC BF575.C35 A77 2020 (print) | DDC
  155.4/124--dc23
LC record available at https://lccn.loc.gov/2018053378

Book design and art direction: Tim Palin Creative
Editorial direction: Kellie M. Hultgren
Music direction: Elizabeth Draper
Music composed and produced by Emily Arrow

Printed in the United States of America.
010220   003099

ACCESS THE MUSIC!

SCAN CODE WITH MOBILE APP

CANTATALEARNING.COM

TIPS TO SUPPORT LITERACY AT HOME

WHY READING AND SINGING WITH YOUR CHILD IS SO IMPORTANT

Daily reading with your child leads to increased academic achievement. Music and songs, specifically rhyming songs, are a fun and easy way to build early literacy and language development. Music skills correlate significantly with both phonological awareness and reading development. Singing helps build vocabulary and speech development. And reading and appreciating music together is a wonderful way to strengthen your relationship.

READ AND SING EVERY DAY!

TIPS FOR USING CANTATA LEARNING BOOKS AND SONGS DURING YOUR DAILY STORY TIME

1. As you sing and read, point out the different words on the page that rhyme. Suggest other words that rhyme.

2. Memorize simple rhymes such as Itsy Bitsy Spider and sing them together. This encourages comprehension skills and early literacy skills.

3. Use the questions in the back of each book to guide your singing and storytelling.

4. Read the included sheet music with your child while you listen to the song. How do the music notes correlate to the words of the song?

5. Sing along on the go and at home. Access music by scanning the QR code on each Cantata book. You can also stream or download the music for free to your computer, smartphone, or mobile device.

Devoting time to daily reading shows that you are available for your child. Together, you are building language, literacy, and listening skills.

Have fun reading and singing!

Have you ever felt **angry** or **worried**? Maybe you didn't get to have a turn while playing a game. Maybe you couldn't fix something that was broken. When we have big **emotions**, it can feel like nothing will help. The feelings are just too big! But if we can **calm down**, we can think of ways to feel better.

One way to calm down is to **check in** with your body by thinking about all of its parts, from your head to your toes. Ready to check in? Turn the page to **breathe** and sing along!

I know how it goes
and you know how it goes
when something's not going right.
Here is something that you can try.

Think about the top of your head.
How does it feel? Checking in!

Move down to your eyes.
How do they feel? Checking in!

So let's breathe in: 1, 2, 3, 4.

Hold it in.

Now let's breathe out: 4, 3, 2, 1.

Try it again.

Let's breathe in: 1, 2, 3, 4.

Hold it in.

Now let's breathe out: 4, 3, 2, 1.

We're calming down by checking in!

Now think about your ears.
What do they hear? Checking in!

Think about the
tip of your nose.
How does it feel?
Checking in!

So let's breathe in: 1, 2, 3, 4.

Hold it in.

Now let's breathe out: 4, 3, 2, 1.

Try it again.

Let's breathe in: 1, 2, 3, 4.

Hold it in.

Now let's breathe out: 4, 3, 2, 1.

We're calming down by checking in!

Think about your shoulders and your neck.
How do they feel? Checking in!

Focus on your belly next.
How does it feel? Checking in!

So let's breathe in: 1, 2, 3, 4.
Hold it in.

Now let's breathe out: 4, 3, 2, 1.
Try it again.

Let's breathe in: 1, 2, 3, 4.
Hold it in.

Now let's breathe out: 4, 3, 2, 1.
We're calming down by checking in!

Now think about your legs:
right and left. Checking in!

Your feet and your toes are last.
How do they feel? Checking in!

So let's breathe in: 1, 2, 3, 4.
Hold it in.

Now let's breathe out: 4, 3, 2, 1.
Try it again.

Let's breathe in: 1, 2, 3, 4.
Hold it in.

Now let's breathe out: 4, 3, 2, 1.
We're calming down by checking in!

SONG LYRICS
Checking In

I know how it goes
and you know how it goes
when something's not going right.
Here is something that you can try.

Think about the top of your head.
How does it feel? Checking in!
Move down to your eyes.
How do they feel? Checking in!

So let's breathe in: 1, 2, 3, 4.
Hold it in.
Now let's breathe out: 4, 3, 2, 1.
Try it again.
Let's breathe in: 1, 2, 3, 4.
Hold it in.
Now let's breathe out: 4, 3, 2, 1.
We're calming down by checking in!

Now think about your ears.
What do they hear? Checking in!
Think about the tip of your nose.
How does it feel? Checking in!

So let's breathe in: 1, 2, 3, 4.
Hold it in.
Now let's breathe out: 4, 3, 2, 1.
Try it again.
Let's breathe in: 1, 2, 3, 4.
Hold it in.

Now let's breathe out: 4, 3, 2, 1.
We're calming down by checking in!

Think about your shoulders and your neck.
How do they feel? Checking in!
Focus on your belly next.
How does it feel? Checking in!

So let's breathe in: 1, 2, 3, 4.
Hold it in.
Now let's breathe out: 4, 3, 2, 1.
Try it again.
Let's breathe in: 1, 2, 3, 4.
Hold it in.
Now let's breathe out: 4, 3, 2, 1.
We're calming down by checking in!

Now think about your legs:
right and left. Checking in!
Your feet and your toes are last.
How do they feel? Checking in!

So let's breathe in: 1, 2, 3, 4.
Hold it in.
Now let's breathe out: 4, 3, 2, 1.
Try it again.
Let's breathe in: 1, 2, 3, 4.
Hold it in.
Now let's breathe out: 4, 3, 2, 1.
We're calming down by checking in!

Checking In

Kindie
Emily Arrow

Intro

I know how it goes and you know how it goes when some-thing's not go - ing right.

Here is some - thing that you can try.

Verse

1. Think a-bout the top of your head. How does it feel? Check-ing in! Move down to your eyes. How do they feel? Check-ing in!

Chorus

So let's breathe in: 1, 2, 3, 4. Hold it in. Now let's breathe out: 4, 3, 2, 1. Try it a-gain.

Let's breathe in: 1, 2, 3, 4. Hold it in. Now let's breathe out: 4, 3, 2, 1. We're calm-ing down by check-ing in!

Verse 2
Now think about your ears.
What do they hear? Checking in!
Think about the tip of your nose.
How does it feel? Checking in!

Chorus

Verse 3
Think about your shoulders and your neck.
How do they feel? Checking in!
Focus on your belly next.
How does it feel? Checking in!

Chorus

Verse 4
Now think about your legs:
right and left. Checking in!
Your feet and your toes are last.
How do they feel? Checking in!

Chorus

GLOSSARY

angry—a strong feeling of being mad

breathe—take in air and blow it out again

calm down—become relaxed or not upset

check in—stop to think about how you feel right now

emotions—feelings, such as happiness or sadness

worried—feeling scared or nervous

CRITICAL THINKING QUESTIONS

1. Think of a time when you felt frustrated, angry, or worried. What was that like? Write about it. When do you think it would be good to breathe and help yourself feel calm? Do you think you might need to calm down for happy emotions, too?

2. Draw a picture of your body and circle the areas we sing about in the book. Where do we start checking in? Where do we finish?

3. Play the song again. Can you count on your fingers from 1 to 4 each time you breathe in and back down from 4 to 1 when you breathe out? Try it with a partner!

TO LEARN MORE

Berube, Kate. *Hannah and Sugar*. New York: Harry N. Abrams Books for Young Readers, 2016.

Coombs, Kate. *Breathe and Be: A Book of Mindfulness Poems*. Boulder, CO: Sounds True, 2017.

Hoena, Blake. *Stretchy Shapes! Straight, Curved, and Twisty*. North Mankato, MN: Cantata Learning, 2019.

Laffin, Jenna. *The Mad Monkey*. North Mankato, MN: Cantata Learning, 2017.

Verde, Susan. *I Am Yoga*. New York: Harry N. Abrams Appleseed, 2015.